AXIOM

ISBN 0 947338 28 4

Copyright © Axiom Publishing
First Edition 1991
Revised Edition 1996
Reprint 1997
Reprinted 1999

Axiom
Australia

Australian
Bush Poems

Contents

Illustrations by Jan Gallehawk

The Song of Australia

There is a land where summer skies
Are gleaming with a thousand dyes,
Blending in witching harmonies,
in harmonies:
And grassy knoll and forest height,
Are flushing in the rosy light,
And all above is azure bright
Australia Australia Australia.

There is a land where honey flows,
Where laughing corn luxuriant grows
Land of the myrtle and the rose,
land of the rose:
On hill and plain the clustering vine,
Is gushing out with purple wine,
And cups are quaffed to thee and thine
Australia Australia Australia.

There is a land where treasures shine
Deep in the dark unfathomed mine,
For worshippers at mammon's shrine,
at mammon's shrine:
Where gold lies hid, and rubies gleam,
And fabled wealth no more doth seem,
The idle fancy of a dream
Australia Australia Australia.

There is a land where homesteads peep
From sunny plain and woodland steep.
And love and joy bright vigils keep,
bright vigils keep:
Where the glad voice of childish glee,
Is mingled with the melody,
Of nature's hidden minstrelsy
Australia Australia Australia.

There is a land where floating free,
From mountain top to girdling sea,
A proud flag waves exultingly, exultingly:
And Freedom's sons the banner bear,
No shackled slave can breathe the air,
Fairest of Britain's daughters fair
Australia Australia Australia.

Caroline Carleton

The Stockman

A bright sun and a loosened rein,
A whip whose pealing sound
Rings forth amid the forest trees
As merrily forth we bound—
As merrily forth we bound, my boys,
And, by the dawn's pale light,
Speed fearless on our horses true
From morn till starry night.

'Oh! for a tame and quiet herd,'
I hear some crawler cry;
But give to me the mountain mob
With the flash of their tameless eye—
With the flash of their tameless eye, my boys,
As down the rugged spur
Dash the wild children of the woods,
And the horse that mocks at fear.

There's mischief in yon wide-horned steer,
There's danger in yon cow;
Then mount, my merry horsemen all,
The wild mob's bolting now—
The wild mob's bolting now, my boys,
But 'twas never in their hides
To show the way to the well-trained nags
That are rattling by their sides.

Oh! 'tis jolly to follow the roving herd
Through the long, long summer day,
And camp at night by some lonely creek
When dies the golden ray.
Where the jackass laughs in the old gum-tree,
And our quart-pot tea we sip;
The saddle was our childhood's home,
Our heritage the whip.

Anonymous

The Wild Colonial Boy

There was a wild colonial boy, Jack Donahoe by name,
Of poor but honest parents he was born in Castlemaine.
He was his father's dearest hope, his mother's pride and joy.
O, fondly did his parents love their Wild Colonial Boy.

Chorus
So ride with me, my hearties, we'll cross the mountains high.
Together we will plunder, together we will die.
We'll wander through the valleys and gallop o'er the plains,
For scorn we to live in slavery, bound down with iron chains!

He was scarcely sixteen years of age when he left his father's home,
A convict to Australia, across the seas to roam.
They put him in the Iron Gang in the Government employ,
But ne'er an iron on earth could hold the Wild Colonial Boy.

And when they sentenced him to hang to end his wild career,
With a shout of defiance bold Danahoe broke clear.
He robbed those wealthy squatters, their stock he did destroy,
But never a trap in the land could catch the Wild Colonial Boy.

Then one day when he was cruising near the broad Nepean's side,
From out the thick Bringelly bush the horse police did ride.
'Die or resign, Jack Donahoe!' they shouted in their joy.
'I'll fight this night with all my might!' cried the Wild Colonial Boy.

He fought six rounds with the horse police before the fatal ball,
Which pierced his heart with cruel smart, caused Donahoe to fall.
And then he closed his mournful eyes, his pistol an empty toy,
Crying: 'Parents dear, O say a prayer for the Wild Colonial Boy.'

Traditional

Bullocky Bill

As I came down Talbingo Hill
I heard a maiden cry,
'There's goes old Bill the Bullocky -
He's bound for Gundagai.'

A better poor old beggar
never cracked an honest crust,
A tougher poor old beggar
Never drug a whip through dust.

His team got bogged on the Five-Mile Creek,
Bill lashed and swore and cried,
'If Nobbie don't get me out of this
I'll tattoo his bloody hide.'

But Nobbie strained and broke the yoke
And poked out the leader's eye,
And the dog sat on the tucker-box
Five miles from Gundagai.

Anon

Freedom on the Wallaby

Our fathers toiled for bitter bread
While idlers thrived beside them;
But food to eat and clothes to wear
Their native land denied them.
They left their native land in spite
Of royalties' regalia,
And so they came, or if they stole
Were sent out to Australia.

They struggled hard to make a home,
Hard grubbing 'twas and clearing.
They weren't troubled much with toffs
When they were pioneering;
And now that we have made the land
A garden full of promise,
Old greed must crook his dirty hand
And come to take it from us.

But Freedom's on the Wallaby,
She'll knock the tyrants silly,
She's going to light another fire
And boil another billy.
We'll make the tyrants feel the sting
Of those that they would throttle;
They needn't say the fault is ours
If blood should stain the wattle.

Henry Lawson

The Shearer's Dream

Oh, I dreamt I shore in a shearin'-shed, and it was a dream of joy,
For every one of the rouseabouts was a girl dressed up as a boy -
Dressed like a page in a pantomime, and the prettiest ever seen -
They had flaxen hair, they had coal-black hair, and every shade between.

There was short, plump girls, there was tall, slim girls,
and the handsomest ever seen;
They was four-foot-five, they was six-foot high, and every height between.

The shed was cooled by electric fans that was over every shoot;
The pens was of polished ma-ho-gany, and everything else to suit,
The huts had springs to the mattresses, and the tucker was simple grand,
And every night by the billabong we danced to a German band.

Our pay was the wool on the jumbucks' backs,
so we shore till all was blue -
The sheep was washed afore they was shore
(and the rams was scented too);
And we all of us wept when the shed cut out,
in spite of the long, hot days,
For every hour them girls waltzed in with whisky and beer on tra-a-a-a-ays!

There was three of them girls to every chap, and as jealous as they could be -
There was three of them girls to every chap, and six of 'em picked on me;
We was drafting' 'em out for the homeward track and sharin'
'em round like steam,
When I woke with my head in the blazin' sun to find '
twas only a shearer's dream.

Henry Lawson

Women of the West

They left the vine-wreathed cottage and the mansion on the hill,
The houses in the busy streets where life is never still,
The pleasure of the city, and the friends they cherished best:
For love they faced the wilderness - the Women of the West.

The roar, and rush, and fever of the city died away,
And the old-time joys and faces - they were gone for many a day;
In their place the lurching coach-wheel, or the creaking bullock-chains,
O'er the everlasting sameness of the never-ending plains.

In the slab-built, zinc-roofed homestead of some lately-settled run,
In the tent beside the bankment of a railway just begun,
In the huts on new selections, in the camps of man's unrest,
On the frontiers of the Nation, live the Women of the West.

The red sun robs their beauty, and, in weariness and pain,
The slow years steal the nameless grace that never comes again;
And there are hours men cannot soothe, and words men cannot say-
The nearest woman's face may be a hundred miles away.

The wide bush holds the secrets of their longing and desires,
When the white stars in reverence light their holy altar-fires,
And silence, like the touch of God, sinks deep into the breast
Perchance He hears and understands the Women of the West.

For them no trumpet sounds to call, no poet plies his arts -
They only hear the beating of their gallant, loving hearts.
But they have sung with silent lives the song all songs above -
The holiness of sacrifice, the dignity of love.

Well have we held our fathers' creed. No call has passed us by.
We faced and fought the wilderness, we sent our sons to die.
And we have hearts to do and dare, and yet, o'er all the rest,
The hearts that made the Nation were the Women of the West.

George Essex Evans

The Overlander

There's a trade you all know well -
It's bringing cattle over -
I'll tell you about the time
When I became a drover.
I made up my mind to try the spec,
To the Clarence I did wander,
And brought a mob of duffers there
To begin as an overlander.

Chorus
Pass the wine cup round, my boys;
Don't let the bottle stand there,
For tonight we'll drink the health
Of every overlander.

When the cattle were all mustered,
And the outfit ready to start,
I saw the lads all mounted,
With their swags left in the cart.
All kinds of men I had
From France, Germany, and Flanders;
Lawyers, doctors, good and bad,
In the mob of overlanders.

From the road I then fed out
Where the grass was green and young;
When a squatter with curse and shout
Told me to move along.
I said 'You're very hard;
Take care, don't raise my dander,
For I'm a regular knowing card
The Queensland overlander.'

'Tis true we pay no licence,
And our run is rather large;
'Tis not often they can catch us,
So they cannot make a charge.
They think we live on store beef,
But no, I'm not a gander;
When a good fat stranger joins the mob,
'He'll do.' says the overlander.

Traditional

Respite

As we went down the ole bush road, George Jones an' me the other day,
His bullicks tuggin' at their load, We didn't have a lot to say;
But by the creek, George looks at me.
Then sorter shakes his head in doubt.
'That ford is runnin' low,' sez he.
'Looks like we're goin' to 'ave a drought.'

Quick on that word my thoughts they flew. Back to a picture of the past:
The drought that came in ninety-two. Full half the countryside to blast.
I seen agen the dyin' stock. The paddicks bare, the trees burned black;
I heard agen the evil flock. Of dark crows cawin' down the track.

I seen full plenty laid to waste. By arid wind and savage sun
Because mankind with sinful haste. Scatters earth's gifts as soon as won.
An' then I felt that sudden fear. That comes to men unsought, unguessed:
'If drought,' I says, 'comes to us here.
In this green place, what of the rest?'

But George, he cocks a weather eye.
Above the trees. Sez he: 'Take heart.
You ain't been noticin' the sky. I reckon somethin's due to start,'
Then sudden music sweet to hear, Came singin' down the forest lane
To make an end to human fear, It was the rain! The blessed rain!

C. J. Dennis

The Swagman and his Mate

From the north to south throughout the year
The shearing seasons run,
The Queensland stations start to shear
When Maoriland has done;
But labour's cheap and runs are wide,
And some the track must tread
From New Year's Day till Christmastide
And never get a shed!
North, west, and south - south, west and north -
They lead and follow fate -
The stoutest hearts that venture forth -
The swagman and his mate.

A restless, homeless class they are
Who tramp in border land.
They take their rest 'neath moon and star -
Their bed the desert sand,
On sunset tracks they ride and tramp,
Till speech has almost died,
And still they drift from camp to camp
In silence side by side.
They think and dream, as all men do;
Perchance their dreams are great -
Each other's thoughts are sacred to
The swagman and his mate.

With scrubs beneath the stifling skies
Unstirred by heaven's breath;
Beyond the Darling Timber lies
A land of living death!
A land that wrong-born poets brave
Till dulled minds cease to grope -
A land where all things perish, save
The memories of hope
When daylight's fingers point out back
(And seem to hesitate)
The far faint dust cloud marks their track
The swagman and his mate.

And one who followed through the scrub
And out across the plain,
And only in a bitter mood
Would see those tracks again; -
Can only write what he has seen -
Can only give his hand -
And greet those mates in words that mean
'I know', 'I understand'.
I hope they'll find the squatter 'white',
The cook and shearers 'straight',
When they have reached the shed to-night -
The swagman and his mate.

Henry Lawson

The Blue Mountains

Above the ashes straight and tall,
Through ferns with moisture dripping,
I climb beneath the sandstone wall,
My feet on mosses slipping.

Like ramparts round the valley's edge
The tinted cliffs are standing.
With many a broken wall and ledge,
And many a rocky landing.

And round about their rugged feet
Deep ferny dells are hidden
In shadowed depths, whence dust and heat
Are banished and forbidden.

The stream that, crooning to itself,
Comes down a tireless rover,
Flows calmly to the rocky shelf,
And there leaps bravely over.

Now pouring down, now lost in spray
When mountain breezes sally,
The water strikes the rock midway,
And leaps into the valley.

Now in the west the colours change,
The blue with crimson blending;
Behind the far Dividing Range,
The sun is fast descending.

And mellowed day comes o'er the place,
And softens ragged edges;
The rising moon's great placid face
Looks gravely o'er the ledges.

Henry Lawson

The Stockmen of Australia

The stockmen of Australia, what rowdy boys are they,
They will curse and swear a hurricane if you come in their way.
They dash along the forest on black, bay, brown, or grey,
And the stockmen of Australia, hard-riding boys are they.

By constant feats of horsemanship, they procure for us our grub,
And supply us with the fattest beef by hard work in the scrub.
To muster up the cattle they cease not night nor day,
And the stockmen of Australia, hard-riding boys are they.

Just mark him as he jobs along, his stockwhip on his knee,
His white mole pants and polished boots and jaunty cabbage-tree.
His horsey-pattern Crimean shirt of colours bright and gay,
And the stockmen of Australia, what dressy boys are they.

If you should chance to lose yourself and drop upon his camp,
He's there reclining on the ground, be it dry or be it damp.
He'll give you hearty welcome, and a stunning pot of tea,
For the stockmen of Australia, good-natured boys are they.

If down to Sydney you should go, and there a stockmen meet,
Mark the sly looks cast on him as he roams through the street.
From the shade of lovely bonnets steal forth those glances gay,
For the stockmen of Australia, the ladies' pets are they.

Whatever fun is going on, the stockmen will be there,
Be it theatre or concert, or dance or fancy fair.
To join in the amusements be sure he won't delay,
For the stockmen of Australia, light-hearted boys are they.

Then here's a health to every lass, and let the toast go round,
To as jolly a set of fellows as ever yet were found.
And all good luck be with them, for ever and today,
Here's to the stockmen of Australia - hip, hip, hooray!

Traditional

The Camp Fire

Reclining near his golden fire,
Alone within the silent bush,
He slowly smokes his evening briar,
And listens to the hovering hush.

The flames are points of falchion-blades,
Light-giving in their wheel and dance;
They gild the underleaf that fades
Above into a glooming trance.

The boles around rise to the night,
Ashen and grey, in solemn-wise,
Opening a heaven of starry light,
Dark violet-blue of nameless dyes.

Thoughts, 'many as the leaves in the woods
Touched by the first autumnal cold,
That fall and lie,' in drifting floods
Draw home with legendary gold.

Fanned, from the fire a burning brand
Lights the bronzed glade with vivid glow;
On earth he whispering lays his hand:
'Mother, to thy calm rest I go.'

Barcroft Boake

Clancy of the Overflow

I had written him a letter which I had, for want of better
Knowledge, sent to where I met him down the Lachlan, years ago,
He was shearing when I knew him, so I sent the letter to him.
Just 'on spec', addressed as follows: 'Clancy of the Overflow'.

And an answer came directed in a writing unexpected.
(And I think the same was written with a thumbnail dipped in tar)
'Twas his shearing mate who wrote it, and verbatim *I will quote it:*
'Clancy's gone to Queensland droving, and we don't know where he are.'

In my wild erratic fancy visions come to me of Clancy
Gone a-droving 'down the Cooper' where the western drovers go;
As the stock are slowly stringing, Clancy rides behind them singing,
For the drover's life has pleasures that the townsfolk never know.

And the bush hath friends to meet him, and their kindly voices greet him
In the murmur of the breezes and the river on its bars,
And he sees the vision splendid of the sunlit plains extended,
And at night the wondrous glory of the everlasting stars.

I am sitting in my dingy little office, where a stingy
Ray of sunlight struggles feebly down between the houses tall,
And the foetid air and gritty of the dusty, dirty city
Through the open window floating, spreads its foulness over all.

And in place of lowing cattle, I can hear the fiendish rattle
Of the tramways and the buses making hurry down the street,
And the language uninviting of the gutter children fighting,
Comes fitfully and faintly through the ceaseless tramp of feet.

And the hurrying people daunt me, and their pallid faces haunt me
As they shoulder one another in their rush and nervous haste,
With their eager eyes and greedy, and their stunted forms and weedy,
For townsfolk have no time to grow, they have not time to waste.

And I somehow rather fancy that I'd like to change with Clancy,
Like to take a turn at droving where the seasons come and go,
While he faced the round eternal of the cashbook and the journal -
But I doubt he'd suite the office, Clancy, of 'The Overflow'.

- A. B. ('Banjo') Paterson

Andy's Gone with Cattle

Our Andy's gone with cattle now—
Our hearts are out of order—
With drought he's gone to battle now
Across the Queensland border.

He's left us in dejection now,
Our thoughts with him are roving;
It's dull on this selection now,
Since Andy went a-droving.

Who now shall wear the cheerful face
In times when things are slackest?
And who shall whistle round the place
When Fortune frowns her blackest?

Oh, who shall cheek the squatter now
When he comes round us snarling?
His tongue is growing hotter now
Since Andy crossed the Darling.

The gates are out of order now,
In storms the 'riders' rattle;
For far across the border now
Our Andy's gone with cattle.

Poor Aunty's looking thin and white;
And Uncle's cross with worry;
And poor old Blucher howls all night
Since Andy left Macquarie.

Oh, may the showers in torrents fall,
And all the tanks run over;
And may the grass grow green and tall
In pathways of the drover;

And may good angels send the rain
On desert stretches sandy;
And when the summer comes again
God grant 'twill bring us Andy.

Henry Lawson

A Thousand Mile Away

Hurrah for the old stock saddle, hurrah for the stock whip too,
Hurrah for the baldy pony, boys, to carry me westward ho;
To carry me westward ho, my boys, that's where the cattle stray,
On the far Barcoo where they eat nardoo, a thousand mile away.

Then give your horses rein, across the open plain;
We'll crack our whips like a thunderbolt, nor care what some folk say;
And a-running we'll bring home them cattle that now roam
On the far Barcoo and the Flinders too, a thousand mile away.

Knee deep in grass we've got to pass, the truth I'm bound to tell,
Where in three weeks the cattle get as fat as they can swell;
As fat as they can swell, my boys, a thousand pound they weigh,
On the far Barcoo and the Flinders too, a thousand mile away.

No Yankee hide e'er grew outside such beef as we can freeze;
No Yankee pastures feed such steers as we send o'er the seas
As we send o'er the seas, my boys, in shipments every day,
From the far Barcoo where they eat nardoo, a thousand mile away.

So put me up with a snaffle, and a four or five inch spur,
And fourteen foot of greenhide whip to chop their flaming fur;
I'll yard them snuffy cattle in a way that's safe to swear,
I'll make them Queensland cattlemen sit back in the saddle and stare.

Hurrah for the old stock saddle, hurrah for the stock whip too,
Hurrah for the baldy pony, boys, to carry me westward ho;
To carry me westward ho, my boys, that's where the cattle stray,
On the far Barcoo where they eat nardoo, a thousand mile away.

Anon

Five Miles from Gundagai

I'm used to punchin' bullock-teams
Across the hills and plains,
I've teamed outback this forty years
In blazin' droughts and rains,
I've lived a heap of troubles down
Without a bloomin' lie,
But I can't forget what happened to me
Five miles from Gundagai.

'Twas gettin' dark, the team got bogged,
The axle snapped in two;
I lost me matches an' me pipe,
So what was I to do?
The rain came on, 'twas bitter cold,
And hungry too was I.
And the dog he shat in the tucker-box,
Five miles from Gundagai.

Some blokes I know has stacks o' luck,
No matter 'ow they fall,
But there was I, Lord love a duck!
No blasted luck at all.
I couldn't make a pot o' tea,
Nor get me trousers dry,
And the dog shat in the tucker-box,
Five miles from Gundagai.

I can forgive the blikin' team,
I can forgive the rain,
I can forgive the dark and cold,
And go through it again.
I can forgive me rotten luck,
But hang me till I die,
I can't forgive that bloody dog
Five miles from Gundagai.

Traditional Version

The Drover's Sweetheart

An hour before the sun goes down
Behind the ragged boughs,
I go across the little run
To bring the dusty cows;
And once I used to sit and rest
beneath the fading dome,
For there was one that I loved best
Who'd bring the cattle home.

Our yard is fixed with double bails;
Round one the grass is green,
The Bush is growing through the rails,
The spike is rusted in;
It was from there his freckled face
Would turn and smile at me;
For he'd milk seven in the race
While I was milking three.

He kissed me twice and once again
And road across the hill;
The pint-pots and the hobble-chain
I hear them jingling still...
About the hut and sunlight fails,
The fire shines through the cracks -
I climb the broken stockyard rails
And watch the bridle-tracks.

And he is coming back again -
He wrote from Evatt's Rock;
A foot-rot in the flock.
The sheep were falling thick and fast
A hundred miles from town,
And when he reached the line at last
He trucked the remnant down.

And so he'll have to stand the cost;
His luck was always bad,
Instead of making more, he lost
The money that he had;
And how he'll manage, heaven knows
(My eyes are getting dim)
He says - he says - he don't - suppose
I'll want - to - marry - him.

As if I wouldn't take his hand
Without a golden glove
Oh' Jack, you men won't understand
how much a girl can love..
I long to see his face once more
Jack's dog! thank God, it's Jack!-
(I never thought I'd faint before)
He's coming - up - the track.

Henry Lawson

Wanderers

As I rose in the early dawn,
While stars were fading white,
I saw upon a grassy slope
A camp-fire burning bright;
With tent behind and blaze before
Three loggers in a row
Sang all together joyously—
Pull up the stakes and go!

As I rode on by Eagle Hawk,
The wide blue deep of air,
The wind among the glittering leaves,
The flowers so sweet and fair,
The thunder of the rude salt waves,
The creek's soft overflow,
All joined in chorus to the words—
Pull up the stakes and go!

Now by the tent on forest skir,
By odour of the earth,
By sight and scent of morning smoke,
By evening camp-fire's mirth,
By deep-sea call and foaming green,
By new stars' gleam and glow,
By summer trails in antique lands—
Pull up the stakes and go!

The world is wide and we are young,
The sounding marches beat,
And passion pipes her sweetest call
In lane and field and street;
So rouse the chorus, brothers all,
We'll something have to show
When death comes round and strikes our tent,
Pull up the stakes and go!

James Hebblethwaite

A Bush Girl

She's milking in the rain and dark,
As did her mother in the past.
The wretched shed of poles and bark,
Rent by the wind, is leaking fast.
She sees the 'home-roof' black and low,
Where, balefully, the hut-fire gleams -
And, like her mother, long ago,
She has her dreams; she has her dreams.

The daybreak haunts the dreary scene,
The brooding ridge, the blue-grey bush,
The 'yard' where all her years have been
Is ankle-deep in dung and slush;
She shivers as the hour drags on,
Her threadbare dress of sackcloth seems;
But, like her mother, years agone,
She has her dreams; she has her dreams.

The sullen 'breakfast' where they cut
The blackened 'junk'. The lowering face,
As though a crime were in the hut,
As though a curse was on the place;
The muttered question and reply,
The tread that shakes the rotting beams,
The nagging mother, thin and dry -
God help the girl! She has her dreams.

Then for "th' separator" start,
Most wretched hour in all her life,
With 'horse' and harness, dress and cart,
No Chinaman would give his 'wife';
Her heart is sick for light and love,
Her face is often fair and sweet,
And her intelligence above
The minds of all she's like to meet.

She reads, by slush-lamp light, maybe,
When she has dragged her dreary round,
And dreams of cities by the sea
(Where butter's up, so much the pound),
Of different men from those she knows,
Of shining tides and broad, bright streams;
Of theatres and city shows,
And her release! She has her dreams.

Could I gain her a little rest,
A little light, if but for one,
I think that it would be the best
Of any good I may have done.
But, after all, the paths we go
Are not so glorious as they seem,
And - if 'twill help her heart to know -
I've had my dream. 'Twas but a dream.

Henry Lawson

Middleton's Rouseabout

Tall and freckled and sandy,
Face of a country lout;
This was the picture of Andy,
Middleton's Rouseabout.

Type of a coming nation,
In the land of cattle and sheep,
Worked on Middleton's station,
'Pound a week and his keep.'

On Middleton's wide dominions
Plied the stockwhip and shears;
Hadn't any opinions,
Hadn't any 'idears'.

Henry Lawson

Jim's Whip

Yes, there it hangs upon the wall
And never gives a sound,
The hand that trimmed its greenhide fall
Is hidden underground,
There, in that patch of sally shade,
Beneath that grassy mound.

I never take it from the wall,
That whip belonged to him,
The man I singled from them all,
He was my husband, Jim;
I see him now, so straight and tall,
So long and lithe of limb.

That whip was with him night and day
When he was on the track;
I've often heard him laugh, and say
That when they heard its crack,
After the breaking of the drought,
The cattle all came back.

And all the time that Jim was here
A-working on the run
I'd hear that whip ring sharp and clear
Just about set of sun
To let me know that he was near
And that his work was done.

I was away that afternoon,
Penning the calves, when, bang!
I heard his whip, 'twas rather soon—
A thousand echoes rang
And died away among the hills,
As toward the hut I sprang.

I made the tea and waited, but,
Seized by a sudden whim,
I went and sat outside the hut
Watching the light grow dim—
I waited there till after dark,
But not a sign of Jim.

The evening air was damp with dew;
Just as the clock struck ten
His horse came riderless—I knew
What was the matter then.
Why should the Lord have singled out
My Jim from other men?

I took the horse and found him where
He lay beneath the sky
With blood all clotted on his hair;
I felt too dazed to cry—
I held him to me as I prayed
To God that I might die.

But sometimes now I seem to hear—
Just when the air grows chill—
A single whip-crack, sharp and clear,
Re-echo from the hill.
That's Jim, to let me know he's near
And thinking of me still.

Barcroft Boake

The Bush

Give us from dawn to dark
Blue of Australian skies,
Let there be none to mark
Whither our pathway lies.

Give us when noontide comes
Rest in the woodland free—
Fragrant breath of the gums,
Cold, sweet scent of the sea.

Give us the wattle's gold
And the dew-laden air,
And the loveliness bold
Loneliest landscapes wear.

These are the haunts we love,
Glad with enchanted hours,
Bright as the heavens above,
Fresh as the wild bush flowers.

James Lister Cuthbertson

Australia's on the Wallaby

Our fathers came to search for gold,
The mine has proved a duffer;
From bankers, boss and syndicate
We always had to suffer.
They fought for freedom for themselves,
Themselves and mates to toil,
But Australia's sons are weary
And the billy's on the boil.

Australia's on the wallaby,
Just listen to the coo-ee;
For the kangaroo, he rolls his swag
And the emu shoulders bluey.
The boomerangs are whizzing round,
The dingo scratches gravel;
The possum, bear and bandicoot
Are all upon the travel,

The cuckoo calls the bats and now
The pigeon and the shag,
The mallee-hen and platypus
Are rolling up their swag;
For the curlew sings a sad farewell
Beside the long lagoon,
And the brolga does his last-way waltz
To the lyrebird's mocking tune.

There's tiger-snakes and damper, boys,
And what's that on the coals?
There's droughts and floods and ragged duds
And dried-up waterholes;
There's shadeless trees and sun-scorched plains,
All asking us to toil;
But Australia's sons are weary
And the billy's on the boil.

Anonymous

The Great Australian Adjective

The sunburnt — stockman stood
And, in a dismal — mood,
Apostrophized his — cuddy;
'The — nag's no — good,
He couldn't earn his — food —
A regular — brumby,
          — !'

He jumped across the — horse
And cantered off, of — course!
The roads were bad and — muddy;
Said he, 'Well, spare me — days
The — Government's — ways
Are screamin' — funny,
          — !'

He rode up hill, down — dale,
The wind it blew a — gale,
The creek was high and — floody.
Said he, 'The — horse must swim,
The same for — me and him,
Is something — sickenin,
          — !'

He plunged into the — creek,
The — horse was — weak,
The stockman's face a — study!
And though the — horse was drowned
The — rider reached the ground
Ejaculating, '—?'
          — !'

W. T. Goodge

Said Hanrahan

'We'll all be rooned,' said Hanrahan
In accents most forlorn
Outside the church ere Mass began
One frosty Sunday morn.

The congregation stood about,
Coat-collars to the ears,
And talked of stock and crops and drought
As it had done for years.

'It's lookin' crook,' said Daniel Croke;
'Bedad, it's cruke, me lad,
For never since the banks went broke
Has seasons been so bad.'

'It's dry, all right,' said young O'Neil,
With which astute remark
He squatted down upon his heel
And chewed a piece of bark.

And so around the chorus ran
'It's keepin' dry, no doubt.'
'We'll all be rooned,' said Hanrahan,
'Before the year is out.

'The crops are done; ye'll have your work
To save one bag of grain;
From here way out to Back-o'-Bourke
They're singin' out for rain.

They're singin' out for rain,' he said,
'And all the tanks are dry.'
The congregation scratched its head,
And gazed around the sky.

'There won't be grass, in any case,
Enough to feed an ass;
There's not a blade on Casey's place
As I came down to Mass.'

'If rain don't come this month,' said Dan,
And cleared his throat to speak—
'We'll all be rooned,' said Hanrahan,
'If rain don't come this week.'

A heavy silence seemed to steal
On all at this remark;
And each man squatted on his heel,
And chewed a piece of bark.

'We want an inch of rain, we do,'
O'Neil observed at last;
But Croke 'maintained' we wanted two
To put the danger past.

'If we don't get three inches, man,
Or four to break this drought,
We'll all be rooned,' said Hanrahan,
'Before the year is out.'

In God's good time down came the rain;
And all the afternoon
On iron roof and window-pane
It drummed a homely tune.

And through the night it pattered still,
And lightsome, gladsome elves
On dripping spout and window-sill
Kept talking to themselves.

It pelted, pelted all day long,
A-singing at its work,
Till every heart took up the song
Way out to Back-o'-Bourke.

And every creek a banker ran,
And dams filled overtop;
'We'll all be rooned,' said Hanrahan,
'If this rain doesn't stop.'

And stop it did, in God's good time:
And spring came in to fold
A mantle o'er the hills sublime
Of green and pink and gold.

And days went by on dancing feet,
With harvest-hopes immense,
and laughing eyes beheld the wheat
Nid-nodding o'er the fence.

And, oh, the smiles on every face,
As happy lad and lass
Through grass knee-deep on Casey's place
Went riding down to Mass.

While round the church in clothes genteel
Discoursed the men of mark,
And each man squatted on his heel,
And chewed his piece of bark.

'There'll be bush-fires for sure, me man,
There will, without a doubt;
We'll all be rooned,' said Hanrahan,
'Before the year is out.'

P. J. Hartigan (John O'Brien)

The Teams

A cloud of dust on the long white road,
And the teams go creeping on
Inch by inch with the weary load;
And by the power of the green-hide goad
The distant goal is won.

With eyes half-shut to the blinding dust,
And necks to the yokes bent low,
The beasts are pulling as bullocks must;
And the shining tires might almost rust
While the spokes are turning slow.

With face half-hid 'neath a broad-brimmed hat
That shades from the heat's white waves,
And shouldered whip with its green-hide plait,
The driver plods with a gait like that
Of his weary, patient slaves.

He wipes his brow, for the day is hot,
And spits to the left with spite;
He shouts at Bally, and flicks at Scot,
And raises dust from the back of Spot,
And spits to the dusty right.

He'll sometimes pause as a thing of form
In front of a settler's door,
And ask for a drink, and remark, 'It's warm,'
Or say, 'There's signs of a thunderstorm,'
But he seldom utters more.

The rains are heavy on roads like these;
And, fronting his lonely home,
For days together the settler sees
The wagons bogged to the axletrees,
Or ploughing the sodden loam.

And then when the roads are at their worst,
The bushman's children hear
The cruel blows of the whips reversed
While bullocks pull as their hearts would burst,
* And bellow with pain,and fear.*

Henry Lawson

Camping

O Scents from dewy grass and tree;
O fluting birds at morn,
Loud, jubilant, or broken-sweet;
O Cloudlets fleecy, torn,
Floating on the fields of azure blue
Far in the distance, low!
I think of these and raptured cry:
Acamping we will go!

With every waft from greening earth
Wet with a gentle shower;
With every moving in the trees;
With every dancing flower;
I hear a song within my breast,
Over wide spaces, and I sigh:
Acamping we will go!

By murmuring streams and fountain falls;
By ferny hills and dales;
By shadowed cleft and hidden cave,
And old forgotten trails;
By bending, perfumed lilied brake;
By waves in endless flow;
I'll sing as on the grass I lie:
Acamping we will go!

By flaming multitudes of stars,
Unvalued of most men,
Offering ephemerals purged might,
Aeries of prison-den;
By crescent moons soaring above
All beauty that I know—
A lover to the bush I'll fly:
Acamping we will go!

Barcroft Boake

The Old Bush Road

Dear old road, wheel-worn and broken,
Winding thro' the forest green,
Barred with shadow and with sunshine,
Misty vistas drawn between.
Grim, scared bluegums ranged austerely,
Lifting blackened columns each
To the large, fair fields of azure,
Stretching ever out of reach.

See the hardy bracken growing
Round the fallen limb of trees;
And the sharp reeds from the marshes,
Washed across the flooded leas;
And the olive rushes, leaning
All their pointed spears to cast
Slender shadows on the roadway,
While the faint, slow wind creeps past.

Ancient ruts grown round with the grasses,
Soft old hollows filled with rain;
Rough, gnarled roots all twisting queerly,
Dark with many a weather-stain.
Lichens moist upon the fences,
Twiners close against the logs;
Yellow fungus in the thickets,
Vivid mosses in the bogs.

Dear old road, wheel-worn and broken,
What delights in thee I find!
Subtle charm and tender fancy,
Like a fragrance in the mind.
Thy old ways have set me dreaming,
And out-lived illusions rise,
And the soft leaves of the landscape
Open on my thoughtful eyes.

See the clump of wattles, standing
Dead and sapless on the rise;
When their boughs were full of beauty,
Even to uncaring eyes,
I was ever first to rifle
The soft branches of their store.
O the golden wealth of blossom
I shall gather there no more!

Now we reach the dun morasses,
Where the red moss used to grow,
Ruby-bright upon the water,
Floating on the weeds below.
Once the swan and wild-fowl glided
By those sedges, green and tall;
Here the blooming bitterns nested;
Here we heard the curlews call.

Climb this hill and we have rambled
To the last turn of the way;
Here is where the bell-birds tinkled
Fairy chimes for me all day.
These were bells that never wearied,
Swung by ringers on the wing;
List! the elfin strains are waking,
Memory sets the bells a-ring!

Dear old road, no wonder, surely,
That I love thee like a friend!
And I grieve to think how surely
All thy simple charm is passing,
And the turmoil of the street
Soon will mar thy sylvan silence
With the tramp of careless feet.

And for this I look more fondly
On the sunny landscape, seen
From the road, wheel-worn and broken
Winding thro' the forest green,
Something still remains of Nature,
Thoughts of other days to bring:—
For the staunch old trees are standing,
And I hear the wild birds sing!

Grace Jennings Carmichael

The Traveller

As I rode in to Burrumbeet,
I met a man with funny feet;
And, when I paused to ask him why
His feet were strange, he rolled his eye
And said the rain would spoil the wheat;
So I rode on to Burrumbeet.

As I rode in to Beetaloo,
I met a man whose nose was blue;
And when I asked him how he got
A nose like that, he answered, 'What
Do bullocks mean when they say 'Moo'?'
So I rode on to Beetaloo.

As I rode in to Ballarat,
I met a man who wore no hat;
And, when I said he might take cold,
He cried, 'The hills are quite as old
As yonder plains, but not so flat.'
So I rode on to Ballarat.

As I rode in to Gundagai,
I met a man and passed him by
Without a nod, without a word.
He turned, and said he'd never heard
Or seen a man wise as I.
But I rode on to Gundagai.

As I rode homeward, full of doubt,
I met a stranger riding out:
A foolish man he seemed to me;
But, 'Nay, I am yourself,' said he,
'Just as you were when you rode out.'
So I rode homeward, free of doubt.

C.J.Dennis

To a Billy

Old billy - battered, brown and black
With many days of camping
Companion of the bulging sack,
And friend in all our tramping:
How often on the Friday night -
Your cubic measure testing -
With jam and tea we stuffed you tight
Before we started nesting!

How often, in the moonlight pale,
Through gums and gullies toiling,
We've been the first the hill to scale,
The first to watch you boiling;
When at the lane the tent was spread
The silver wattle under,
And early shafts of rosy red
Clefts sea-born mists asunder!

And so, old Billy, you recall
A host of sunburnt faces,
And bring us back again to all
The best of camping places.
True flavour of the bush you bear
Of camp and its surrounding.
Of freedom and of open air,
Of healthy life abounding.

James L Cuthbertson

Where the Pelican Builds

The horses were ready, the rails were down
But the riders lingered still -
One had a parting word to say,
And one had his pipe to fill.
Then they mounted, one with a granted prayer,
And one with a grief unguessed.
'We are going', they said as they rode away,
'Where the pelican builds her nest!'

They had told us of pastures wide and green,
To be sought past the sunset's glow;
Of rifts in the ranges by opal lit;
And gold 'neath the river's flow.
And thirst and hunger were banished words
When they spoke of that unknown West;
No droughts they dreaded, no flood they feared,
Where the pelican builds her nest!

The creek at the ford was but fetlock deep
When we watched them crossing there;
The rains have replenished it thrice since then,
And thrice has the rock lain bare.
But the waters of Hope have flowed and fed,
And never from blue hill's breast
Come back - by the sun and the sands devoured
Where the pelican builds her nest.

Mary Hannay Foott

The Swagman

Oh, he was old and he was spare;
His bushy whiskers and his hair
Were all fussed up and very grey;
He said he'd come a long, long way
And had a long, long way to go.
Each boot was broken at the toe,
And he'd a swag upon his back.
His billy-can, as black as black,
Was just the thing for making tea
At picnics, so it seemed to me.

'Twas hard to earn a bite of bread,
He told me. Then he shook his head,
All the little corks that hung
Around his hat-brim danced and swung
And bobbed about his face; and when
I laughed he made them dance again.
He said they were for keeping flies—
'The pesky varmints'—from his eyes.
He called me 'Codger'... 'Now you see
The best days of your life,' said he.
"But days will come to bend your back,
And, when they come, keep off the track.
Keep off, young codger, if you can.'

He seemed a funny sort of man.
He told me that he wanted work,
But jobs were scarce this side of Bourke,
And he supposed he'd have to go
Another fifty mile or so.
'Nigh all my life the track I've walked,'
He said. I liked the way he talked.
And oh, the places he had seen!
I don't know where he had not been—
On every road, in every town,
All through the country, up and down.
'Young codger, shun the track,' he said.
I noticed then that his old eyes
Were very blue and very wise.
'Ay, once I was a little lad,'
He said, and seemed to grow quite sad.

I sometimes think: When I'm a man,
I'll get a good black billy-can
And hang some corks around my hat,
And lead a jolly life like that.

C.J.Dennis

In Possum Land

In Possum Land the nights are fair,
The streams are fresh and clear;
No dust is in the moonlit air,
No traffic jars the ear.

With possums gambolling overhead,
'Neath western stars so grand,
Ah! would that we could make our bed
To-night in Possum Land.

Henry Lawson

The Man From Snowy River

There was a movement at the station, for the word had passed around
That the colt from Old Regret had got away,
And had joined the wild bush horses - he was worth a thousand pounds.
So all the cracks had gathered to the fray.
All the tried and noted riders from the stations near and far
had mustered at the homestead overnight,
For the bushmen love hard riding where the wild bush horses are,
And the stock-horse snuffs the battle with delight.

There was Harrison, who made his pile when Pardon won the cup,
The old man with his hair as white as snow;
But few could ride beside him when his blood was fairly up -
He would go wherever horse and man could go.
And Clancy of the Overflow came down to lend a hand,
No better horseman ever held the reins;
For never horse could throw him while the saddle-girths would stand -
He learnt to ride while droving on the plains.

And one was there, a stripling on a small and weedy beast;
He was something like a racehorse undersized,
With a touch of Timor pony - three parts thoroughbred at least -
And such as are by mountain horsemen prized.
He was hard and tough and wiry - just the sort that won't say die -
There was courage in his quick impatient tread;
And he bore the badge of gameness in his bright and fiery eye,
And the proud and lofty carriage of his head.

But still so slight and weedy, one would doubt his power to stay,
And the old man said, - 'That horse will never do
For a long and tiring gallop - lad, you'd better stop away,
Those hills are far too rough for such as you.'
So he waited, sad and wistful - only Clancy stood his friend -
'I think we ought to let him come,' he said;
'I warrant he'll be with us when he's wanted at the end,
For both his horse and he are mountain bred.

'He hails from Snowy River, up by Kosciusko's side,
Where the hills are twice as steep and twice as rough;
Where a horse's hoofs strike firelight from the flintsones every stride,
The man that holds his own is good enough.
'And the Snowy River riders on the mountains strike their home,
Where the river runs those giant hills between;
I have seen full many a horseman since I first commenced to roam,
But nowhere yet such horsemen have I seen.'

So he went; they found the horses by the big mimosa clump,
They raced away towards the mountain's brow,
And the old man gave his orders, 'Boys go at them from the jump,
No use to try for fancy riding now.
And, Clancy, you must wheel them, try and wheel them to the right.
Ride boldly, lad, and never fear the spills,
For never yet was rider that could keep the mob in sight,
If once they gain the shelter of those hills.'

So Clancy rode to wheel them - he was racing on the wing
Where the best and boldest riders take their place,
And he raced his stock-horse past them, and he made the ranges ring
With the stockwhip , as he met them face to face.
Then they halted for a moment, while he swung the dreaded lash,
But they saw their well-loved mountain full in view,
And they charged beneath the stockwhip with a sharp and sudden dash,
And off into the mountain scrub they flew.

Then fast the horsemen followed, where the gorges deep and black.
Resounded to the thunder of their tread,
And the stockwhips woke the echoes, and they fiercely answered back
From cliffs and crags that beetled overhead.
And upward, ever upward, the wild horses held their way,
Where mountain ash and kurrajong grew wide;
And the old man muttered fiercely, 'We may bid the mob good-day,
No man can hold them down the other side.'

When they reached the mountain's summit, even Clancy took a pull -
It well might make the boldest hold their breath;
The wild hop scrub grew thickly, and the hidden ground was full
Of wombat holes, and any slip was death.
But the man from Snowy River let the pony have his head,
And he swung his stockwhip round and gave a cheer,
And he raced him down the mountain like a torrent down its bed
While the others stood and watched in very fear.

He sent the flint-stones flying, but the pony kept his feet,
He cleared the fallen timber in his stride,
And the man from Snowy River never shifted in his seat -
It was grand to see that mountain horseman ride.
Through the stringybarks and saplings, on the rough and broken ground,
Down the hillside at a racing pace he went;
And never drew the bridle till he landed safe and sound
At the bottom of that terrible descent.

He was right among the horses as they climbed the farther hill,
And the watchers on the mountain, standing mute,
Saw him ply the stockwhip fiercely; he was right among them still,
As he raced across the clearing in pursuit.
Then they lost him for a moment, where two mountain gullies met
In the ranges - but a final glimpse reveals
On a dim and distant hillside the wild horses racing yet,
With the man from Snowy River at their heels.

And then he ran them single-handed till their sides were white with foam;
He followed like a bloodhound on their track,
Till they halted, cowed and beaten; then he turned their heads for home,
And alone and unassisted brought them back.
But his hardy mountain pony he could scarcely raise a trot,
He was blood from hip to shoulder from the spur;
But his pluck was still undaunted, and his courage fiery hot,
For never yet was mountain horse a cur.

And down by Kosciusko, where the pine-clad ridges raise
Their torn and rugged battlements on high,
Where the air is clear as crystal, and the white stars fairly blaze
At midnight in the cold and frosty sky;
And where around the Overflow the reed-beds sweep and sway
To the breezes, and the rolling plains are wide,
The Man from Snowy River is a household word today,
And the stockmen tell the story of his ride.

A. B. ('Banjo') Paterson

The Bush Girl

So you rode from the range where your brothers select,
Through the ghostly, grey Bush in the dawn -
You rode slowly at first, lest her heart should suspect
That you were so glad to be gone;
You had scarcely the courage to glance back at her
By the homestead receding from view,
And your breathed with relief as you rounded the spur,
For the world was a wide world to you.

Grey eyes that grow sadder than sunset or rain,
Fond heart that is ever more true,
Firm faith that grows firmer for watching in vain -
She'll wait by the sliprails for you.

Ah! the world is new and a wide one to you,
But the world to your sweetheart is shut,
For a change never comes to the lonely Bush homes
Of the stockyard, the scrub, and the hut;
And the only relief from its dulness she feels
When the ridges grow softened and dim,
And away in the dusk to the sliprails she steals
To dream of past hours 'with him'.

Do you think, where, in place of bare fences, dry creeks,
Clear streams and green hedges are seen -
Where the girls have the lily and rose in their cheeks,
And the grass in mid-summer is green -
Do you think, now and then, now or then, in the whirl
Of the town life, while London is new,
Of the hut in the Bush and the freckled-faced girl
Who waits by the sliprails for your?

Grey eyes that are sadder than sunsets or rain,
Bruised heart that is ever more true,
Fond faith that is firmer for trusting in vain -
She waits by the sliprails for you.

Henry Lawson

The Shearing-Shed

'The ladies are coming,' the super says
To the shearers sweltering there,
And 'the ladies' means in the shearing-shed:
'Don't cut 'em too bad. Don't swear.'
The ghost of a pause in the shed's rough heart,
And lower is bowed each head;
Then nothing is heard save a whispered word
And the roar of the shearing-shed.

The tall, shy rouser has lost his wits;
His limbs are all astray;
He leaves a fleece on the shearing-board
And his broom in the shearer's way.
There's a curse in store for that jackeroo
As down by the wall he slants—
But the ringer bends with his legs askew
And wishes he'd 'patched them pants'.

They are girls from the city. Our hearts rebel
As we squint at their dainty feet,
While they gush and say in a girly way
That 'the dear little lambs' are 'sweet'.
And Bill the Ringer, who'd scorn the use
Of a childish word like damn,
Would give a pound that his tongue were loose
As he tackles a lively lamb.

Swift thought of home in the coastal towns—
Or rivers and waving grass—
And a weight on our hearts that we cannot define
That comes as the ladies pass;
But the rouser ventures a nervous dig
With his thumb in the next man's back;
And Bogan says to his pen-mate: 'Twig
The style of that last un, Jack.'

Jack Moonlight gives her a careless glance—
Then catches his breath with pain;
His strong hand shakes, and the sunbeams dance
As he bends to his work again.
But he's well disguised in a bristling beard,
Bronzed skin, and his shearer's dress;
And whatever he knew or hoped or feared
Was hard for his mates to guess.

Jack Moonlight, wiping his broad, white brow,
Explains, with a doleful smile,
'A stitch in the side,' and 'I'm all right now'—
But he leans on the beam awhile,
And gazes out in the blazing noon
On the clearing, brown and bare...
She had come and gone—like a breath of June
In December's heat and glare.

Henry Lawson

Old Man Platypus

Far from the trouble and toil of town,
Where the reed beds sweep and shiver,
Look at a fragment of velvet brown -
Old Man Platypus drifting down,
Drifting along the river.

And he plays and dives in the river bends
In a style that is most elusive;
With few relations and fewer friends,
For Old Man Platypus descends
From a family most exclusive

He shares his burrow beneath the bank
With his wife and his son and daughter
At the roots of the reeds and the grasses rank;
And the bubbles show where our hero sank
To its entrance under water.

Safe in their burrow below the falls
They live in a world of wonder,
Where no one visits and no one calls,
They sleep like little brown billiard balls
With their beaks tucked neatly under.

And he talks in a deep unfriendly growl
As he goes on his journey lonely;
For he's no relation to fish or fowl,
Nor to bird nor beast, nor to horned owl;
In fact, he's the one and only!

A B (Banjo) Paterson

O Cupid, Cupid; Get Your Bow!

Ariding down along the stream,
Along the sparkling water,
And past the pool where lilies gleam,
There comes the squatter's daughter.

Her eyes are kind; her lips are warm;
And like a flower her face is;
The habit shows her bonny form
As graceful as a Grace's.

O I'll be mad of love, I know;
My head she'll surely addle;
O Cupid, Cupid, Get your bow;
And shoot her from the saddle!

For, like a bird on breezes waft,
She quickly, quickly passes;
O Cupid, Cupid, draw your shaft;
And bring her to the grasses!

O she is worthy game for you;
And there is none to match her.
So, Cupid, send your arrow true;
And I'll be there to catch her!

Henry Lawson